ANTICIPATION

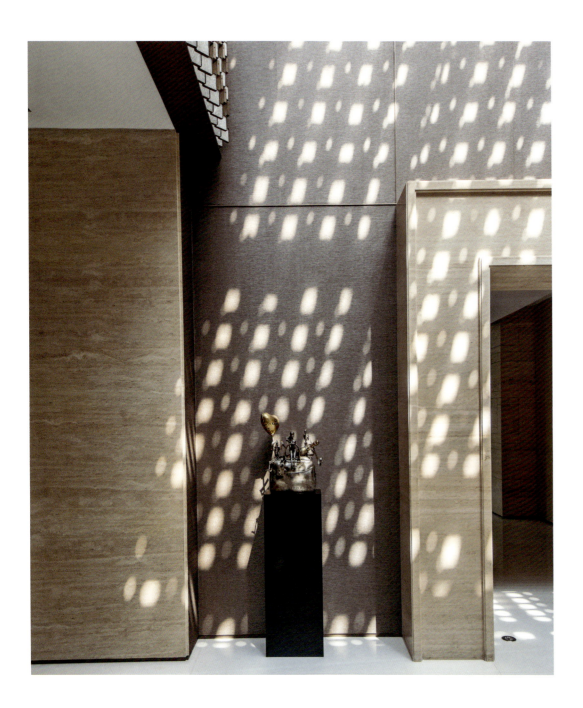

THOMAS ELLIOTT **DIRECTIONS**

images
Publishing

COLLECTIVE SPACES AND SANCTUARIES

public adjective or noun

pu·blic ˈpə-blik

adjective

1 relates to being open or exposed, or being prominent

2 used to describe areas that are provided for everyone to use,
 or where you can easily be seen and heard

noun

1 the people as a whole, in general and universal

2 a group of people having common interests or characteristics
 for a particular event or activity

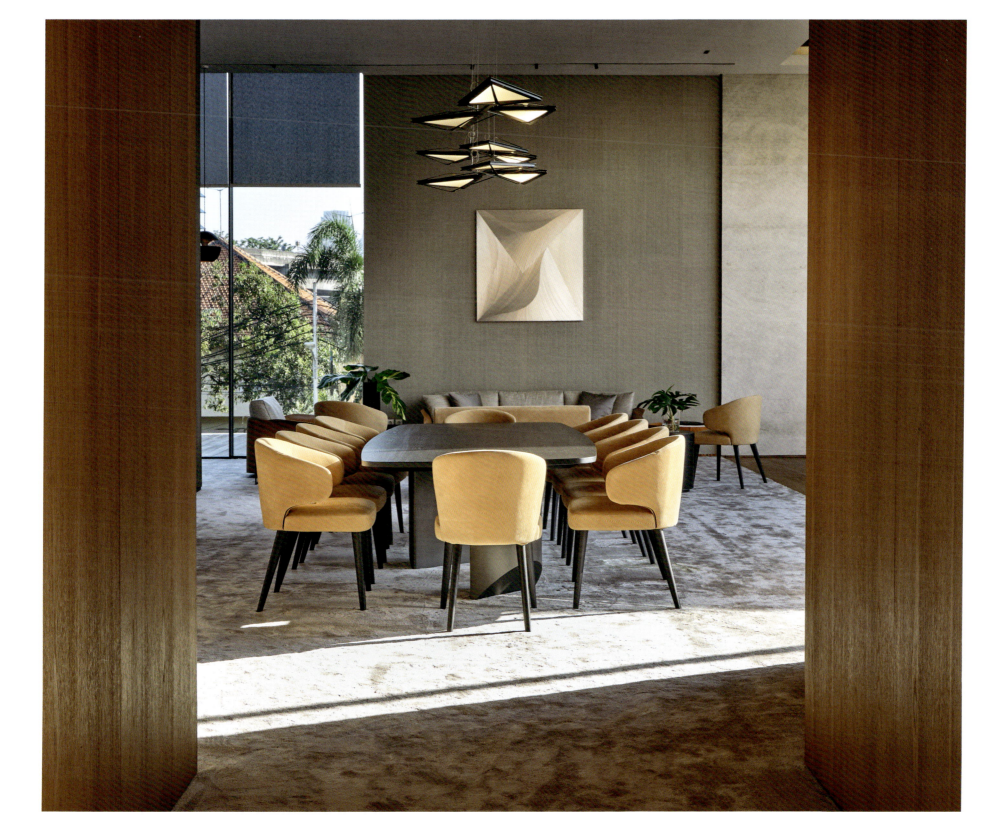

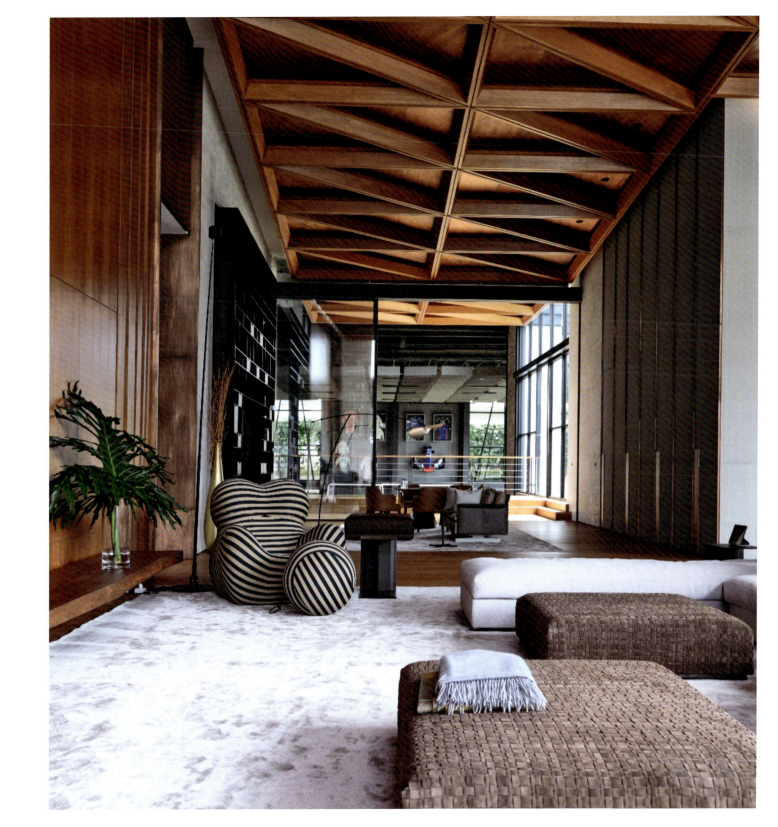

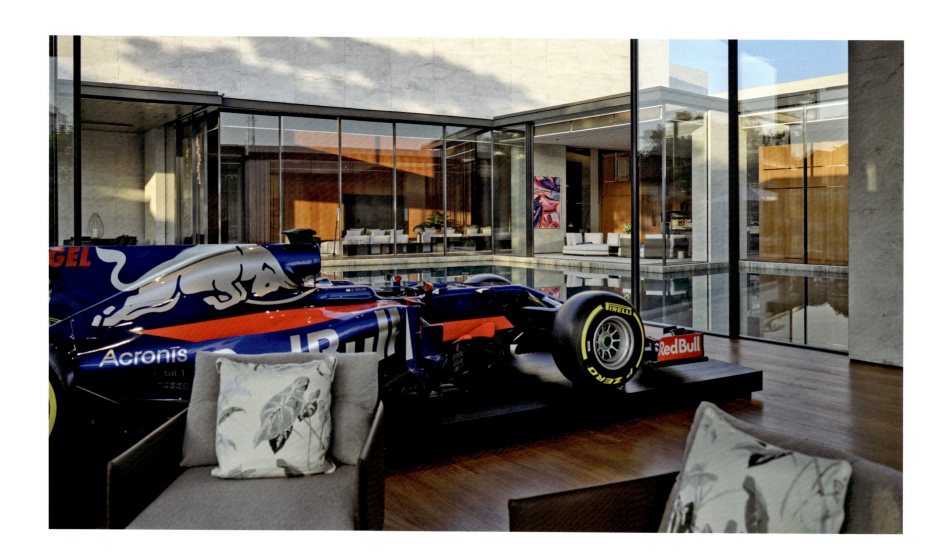

private adjective or noun

pri·vate ˈprī-vət

adjective

1   restricted to or for the use of one particular person or group
    of people
2   not open to the public
3   (of a person) having no official or public role or position
4   belonging to or for the use of one particular person or group
    of people only

noun

1   not holding public office or employment
2   a person in the military of the lowest rank, below a corporal
3   a person of low rank in any of various organizations (such as a
    police or fire department)

transition noun or verb

tran·si·tion tran(t)-ˈsi-shən

noun | plural: transitions

1 process of a shift or change from one state, subject, place, to another

2 a phase or period during which a change or shift is happening

3 something that links one state, subject, place, and so on, to another; a connecting part or piece

4 a passage of discourse in which a shift (as of subject or location) is effected, such as a segment connecting two sections of one piece, for example, in music (the bridge; a musical modulation)

verb | transitions; transitioning; transitioned

1 make a shift or change from one state, subject, place, and so on, to another; to make a transition

2 to cause (something or someone) to change or shift from one state, subject, place, and so on, to another

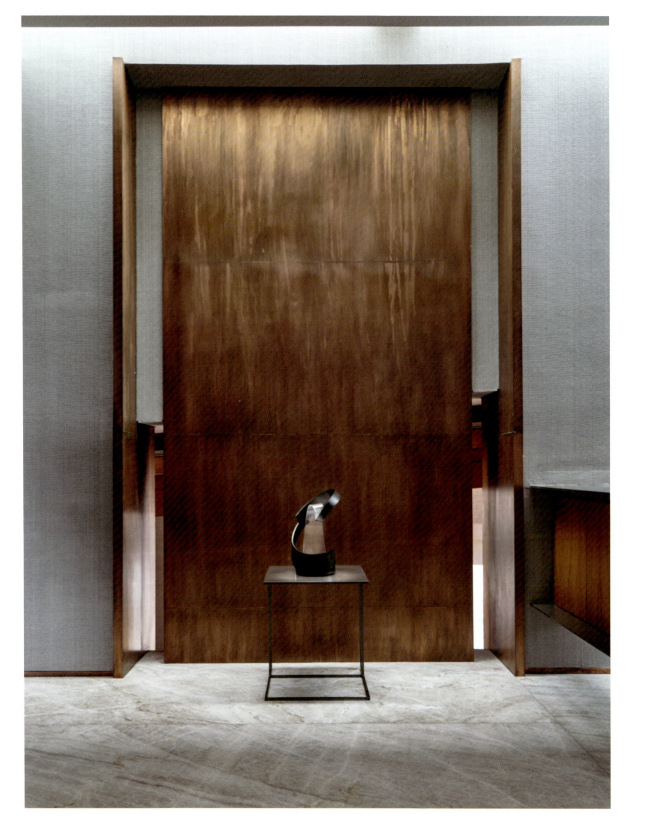

sanctuary noun or adjective

sanc·tu·ary ˈsaŋ(k)-chə-ˌwer-ē

noun

1 a place where people who are in danger can go to be safe, or where people can be provided with shelter, refuge, or protection

2 the most sacred part of a religious building (such as where the altar is placed within a Christian church)

3 a place protected by law where birds, animals, and other wildlife are protected and can live and breed without interferene; and where predators are controlled and hunting is illegal

4 the immunity from law attached to a sanctuary

adjective

1 relates to being a jurisdiction, municipality, or locality that provides limited cooperation to federal officials in the enforcement of immigration laws or policies

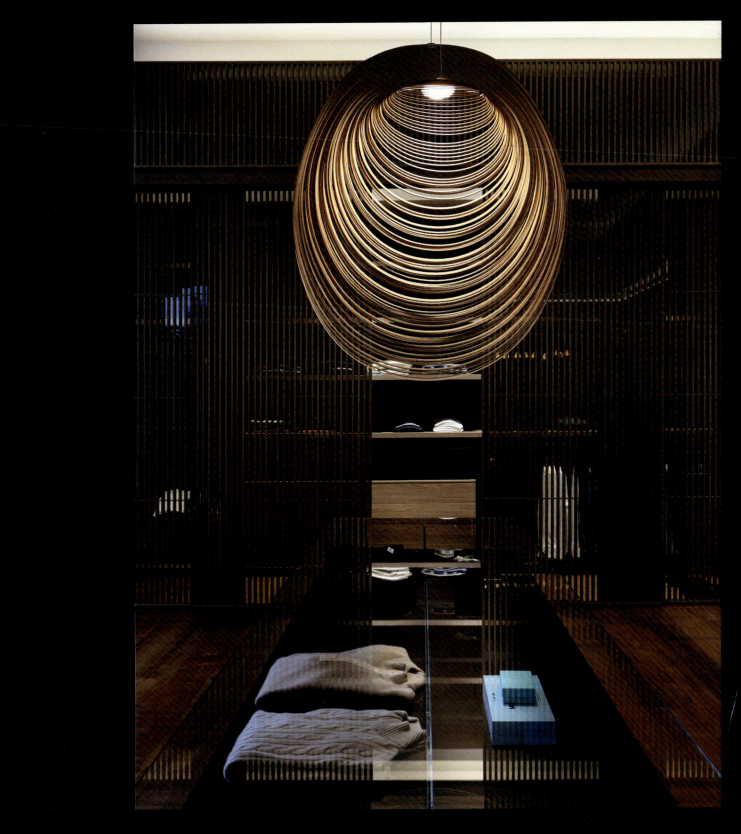

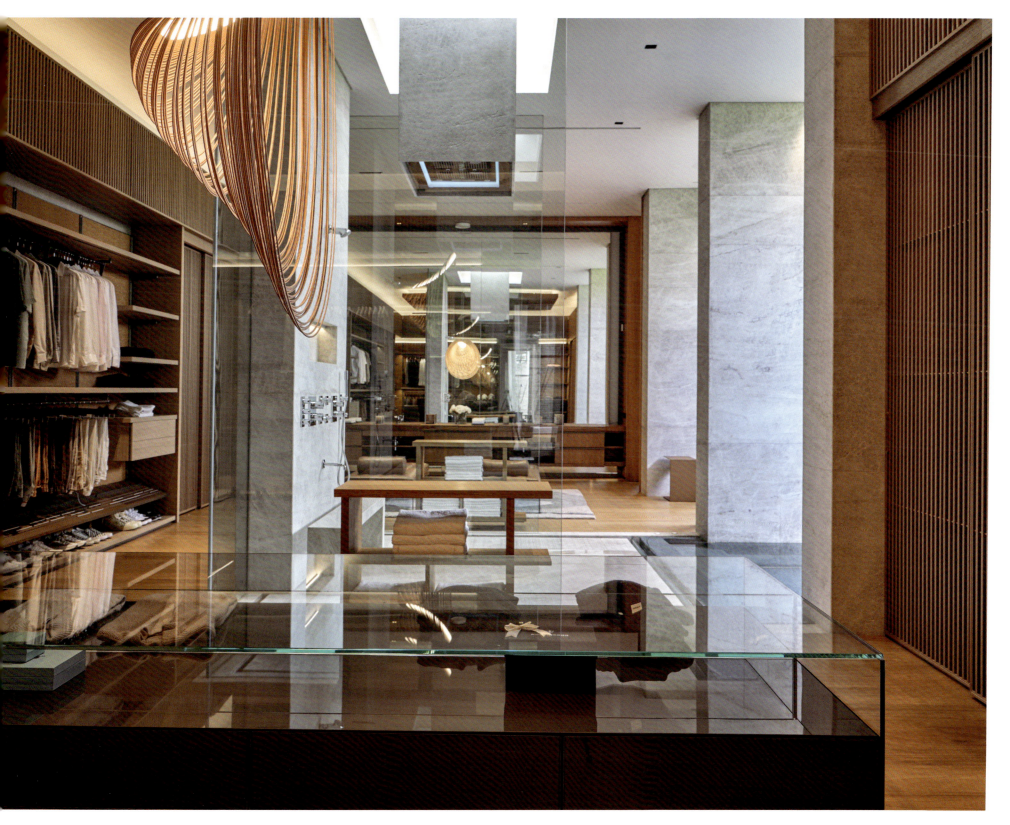

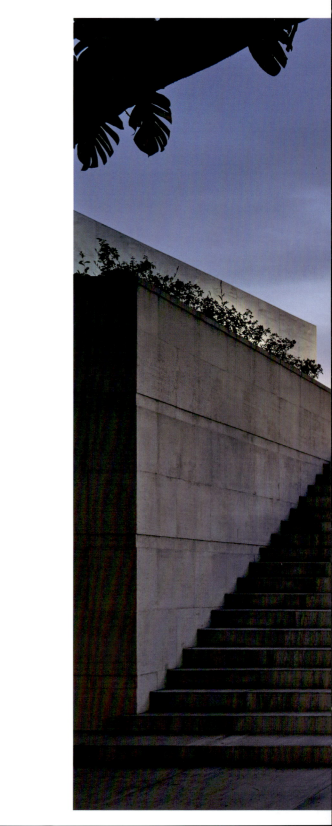

anticipation noun

an·tic·i·pa·tion (ˌ)an-ˌti-sə-ˈpā-shən

1   the act of looking forward to something with a hopeful or eager
     excitement, a feeling of pleasurable expectation
2   the visualization of a future event or state, or a prior action or
     form that expects a later type
3   in music, the early sounding of one or more unstressed,
     usually short, notes or tones of a succeeding chord to form a
     temporary dissonance

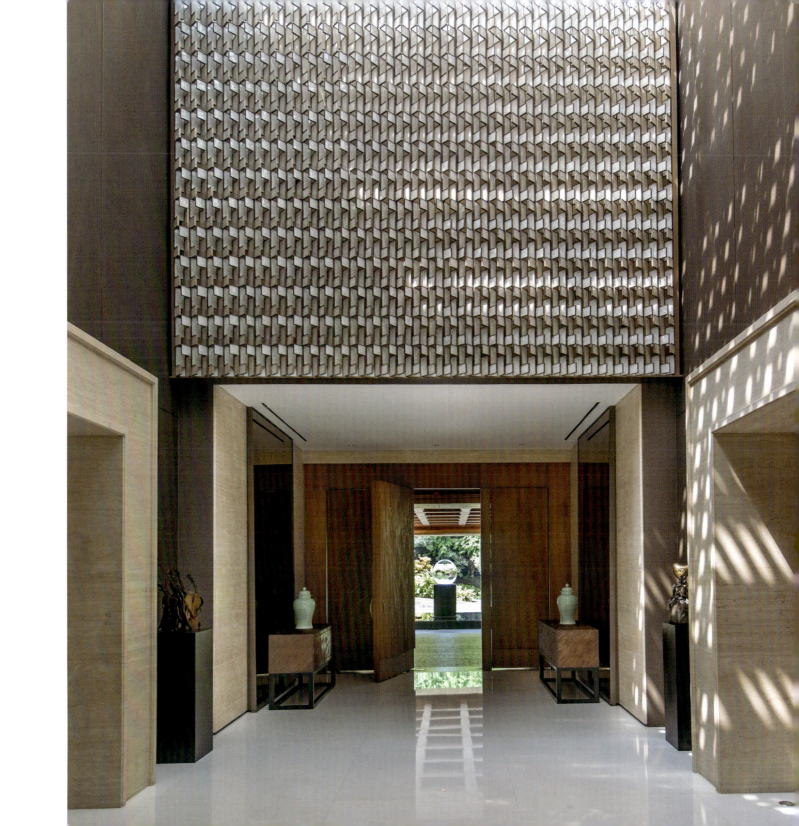

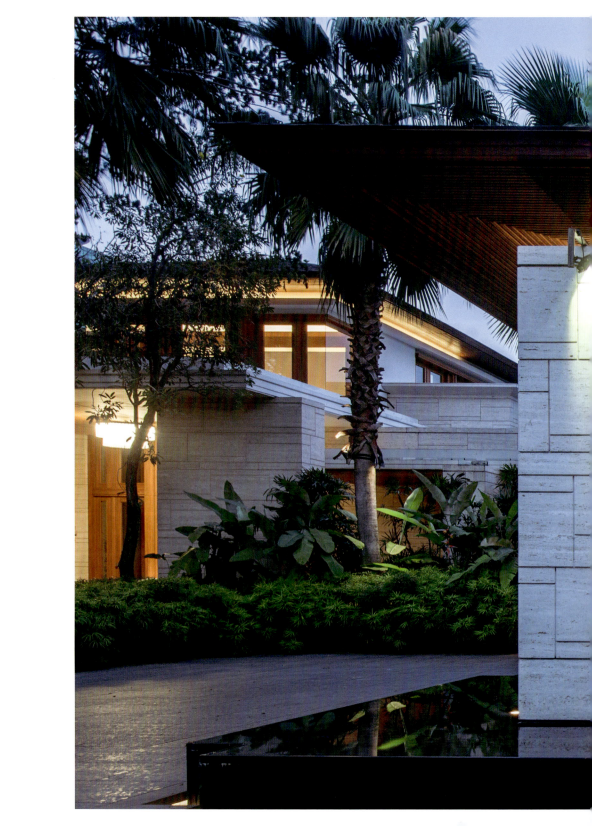

CAPTURING LIGHT

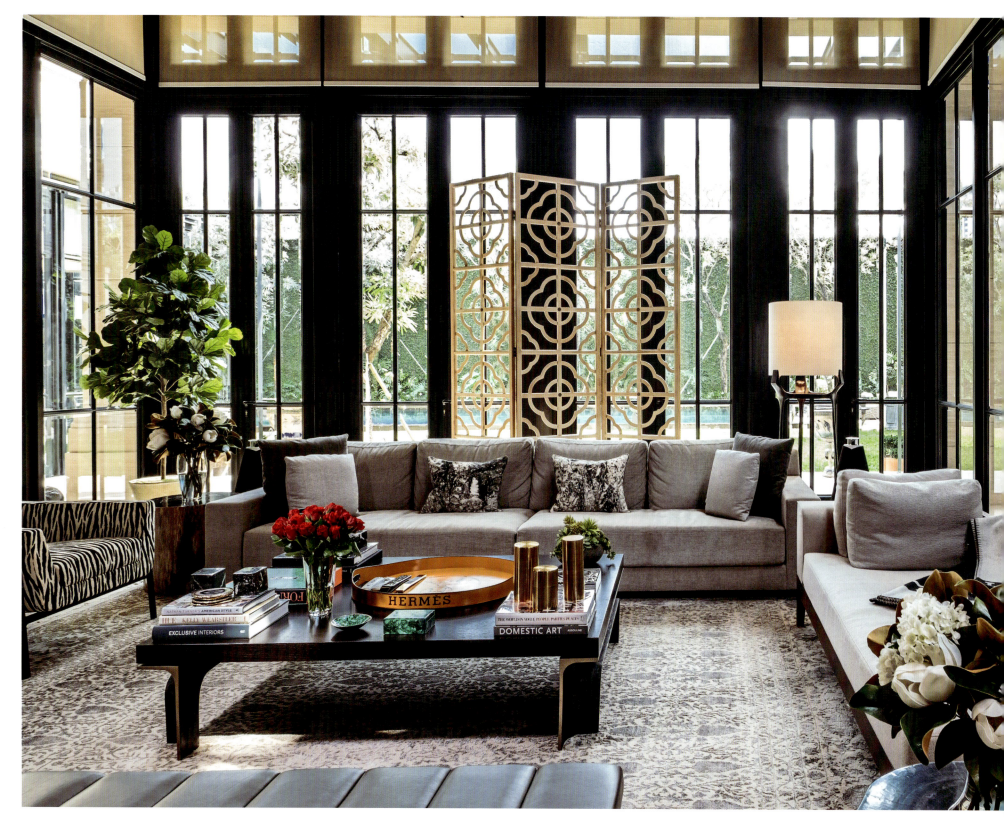

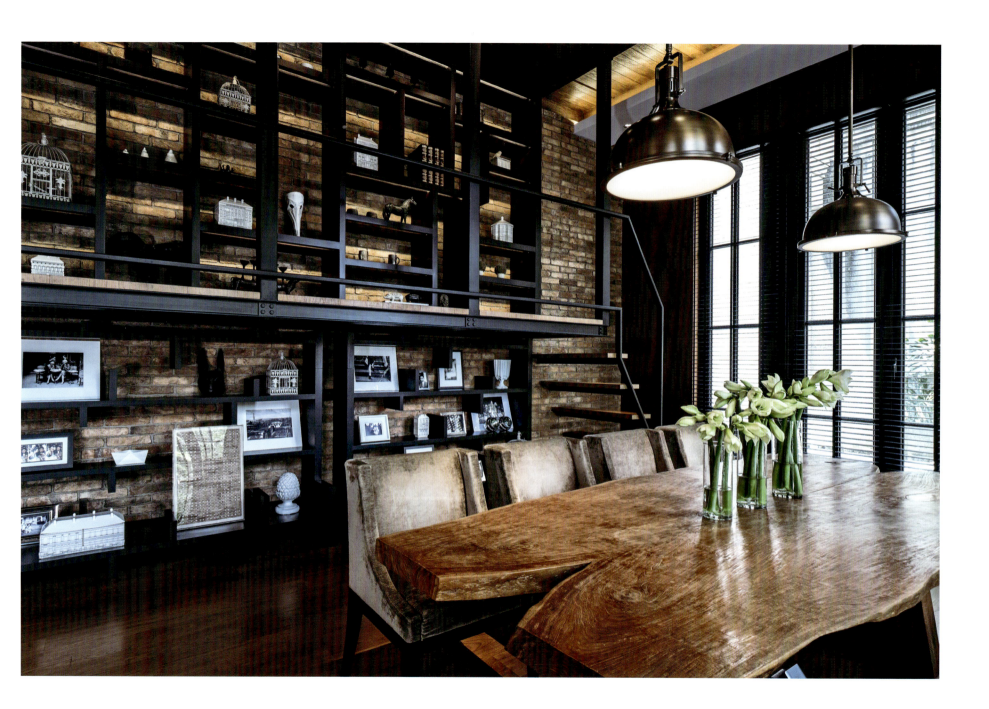

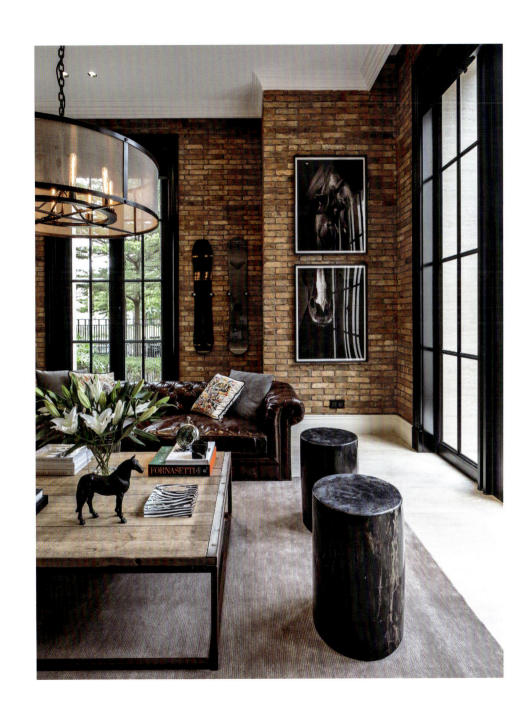

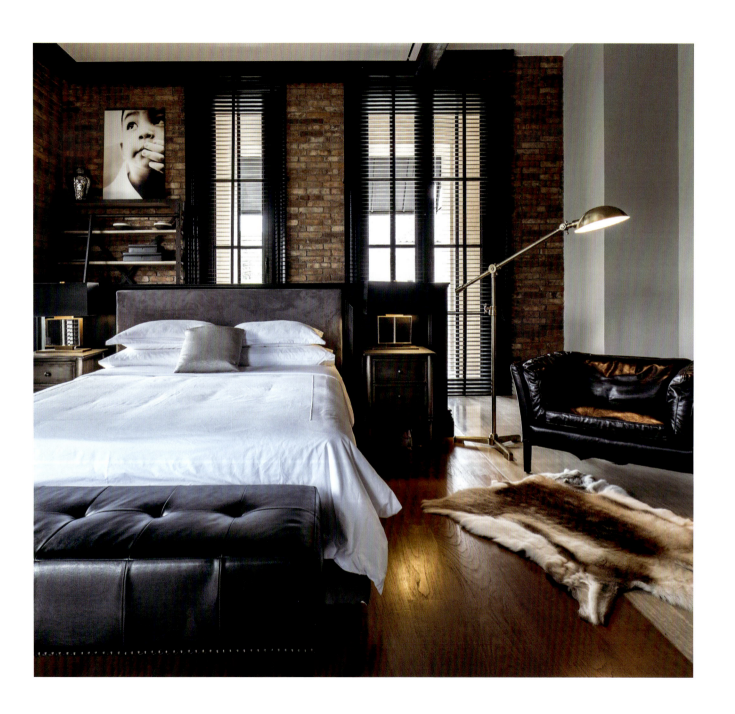

in-between adjective or noun

in·be·tween ˌin-bi-ˈtwēn

adjective

1 situated or being in the space that separates two contrasting conditions or categories, in the sense of an interval

2 describes the intermediate stage or perceived position bounded by two or more points in space, time, or sequence, such as on an imaginary line connecting two extremes or points

noun

1 a thing that (or person who) is considered to be an intermediate

in between prepositional phrase

in be·tween ˌin-bi-ˈtwen

1 describes when something or someone is in a place that is between two or more things

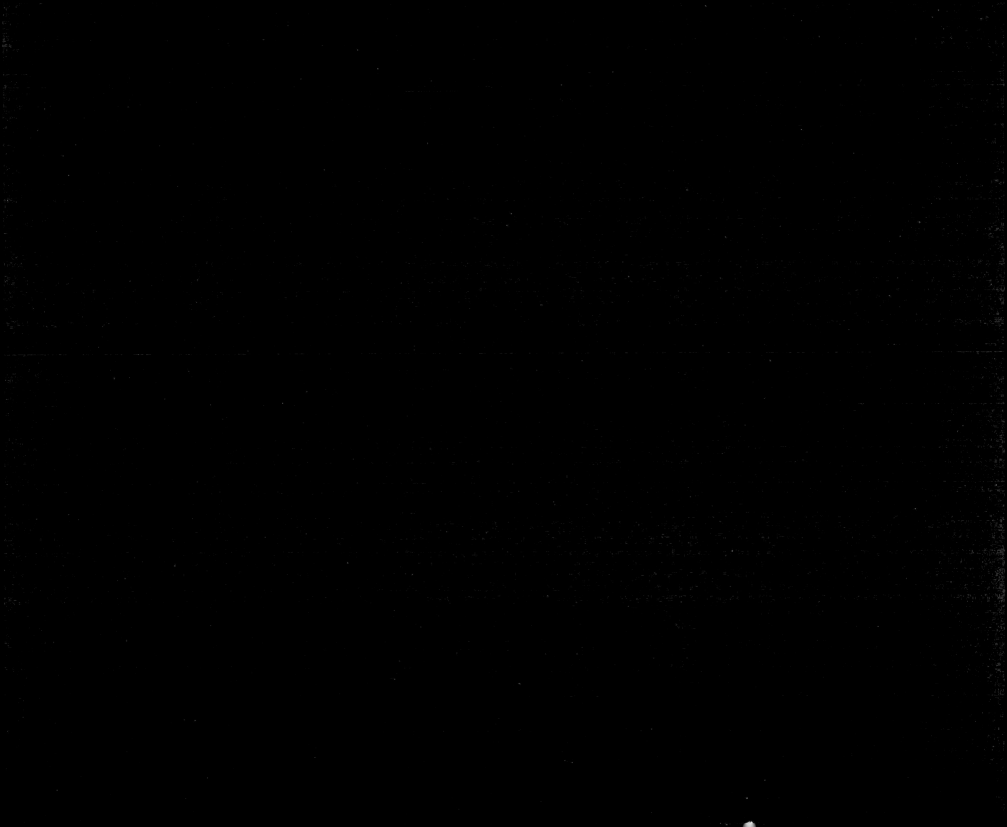

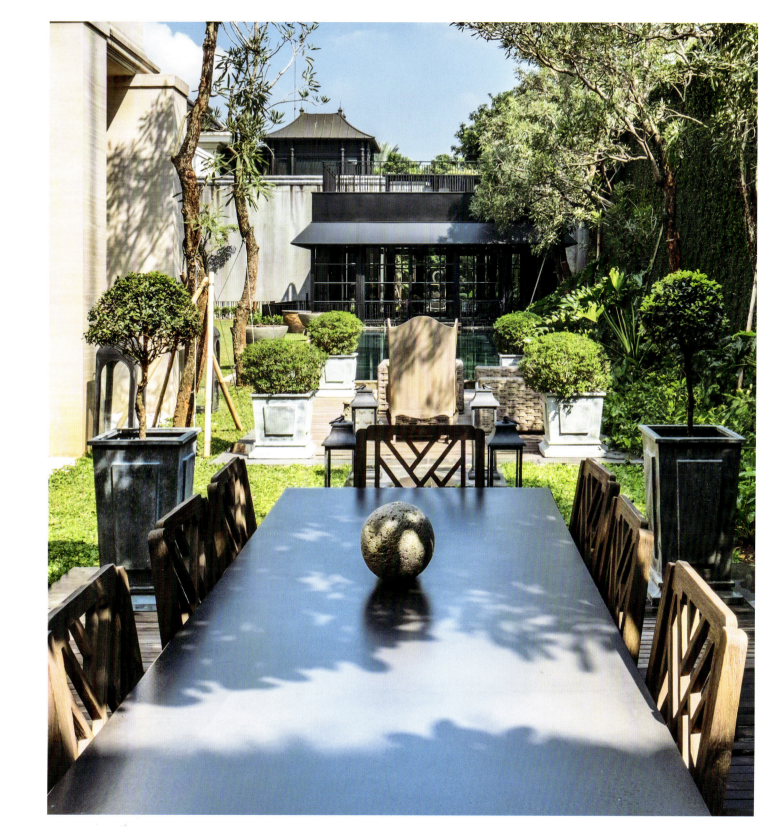

FRAMING NATURE

TRANSITIONAL STORIES

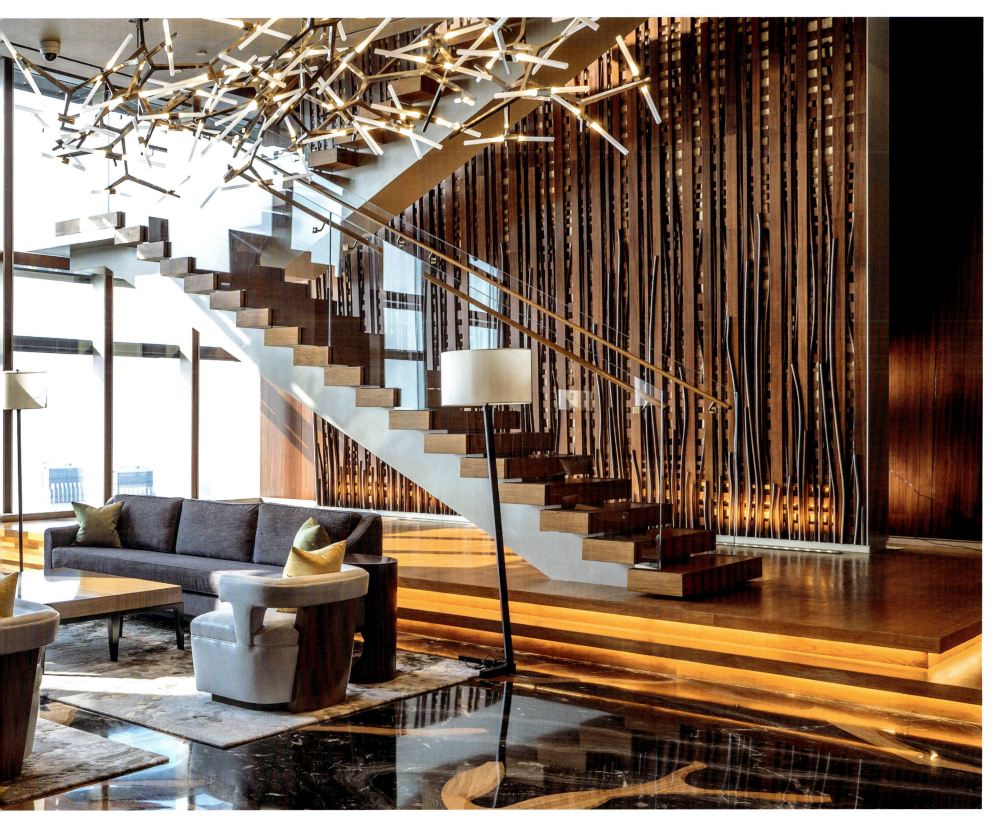

root noun or verb

ˈrüt

noun | plural: roots

1   the part of a plant or tree, which typically grows downward into the soil, fixing the plant as a means of anchorage and support, and drawing nutriment and moisture from the ground; it differs from a stem especially in lacking nodes, buds, and leaves

2   any subterranean plant part (such as a true root or a bulb, tuber, rootstock, or other modified stem), especially when fleshy and edible, and which functions as an organ of absorption, aeration, and food storage

3   any underground part of a plant, as a rhizome

4   the initial segment of a spinal nerve where it branches from the spinal cord; nerve root

5   the part of an organ or physical structure by which it is attached to the body, such as the part of a tooth within the socket

6   a person or family as the source of offspring or descendants

7   a close relationship with an environment or a person's real or true home: *her roots (plural)*

8   the part by which an object is attached to something else

9   an underlying support or the lower part; base

10 the source or origin of a thing (as of a condition or quality)

11 the fundamental or essential part; at the heart—often used in the phrase *at the root of*

12 in music, the fundamental note of a chord or of a series of harmonies

13 the simple element inferred as the basis from which a word is derived by phonetic change or by extension (such as composition or the addition of an affix or inflectional ending)

verb | roots; rooting; rooted

1 to furnish with or enable to develop roots
2 to fix or implant by or as if by roots
3 to remove altogether by or as if by pulling out by the roots
4 to have an origin or base; to grow roots or take root
5 to turn up the earth or soil with the snout, such as a swine
6 to poke or dig about
7 to turn over, dig up, or discover and bring to light
8 to noisily cheer, to give encouragement, or applaud a contestant or team
9 to wish the success of or lend support to someone or something

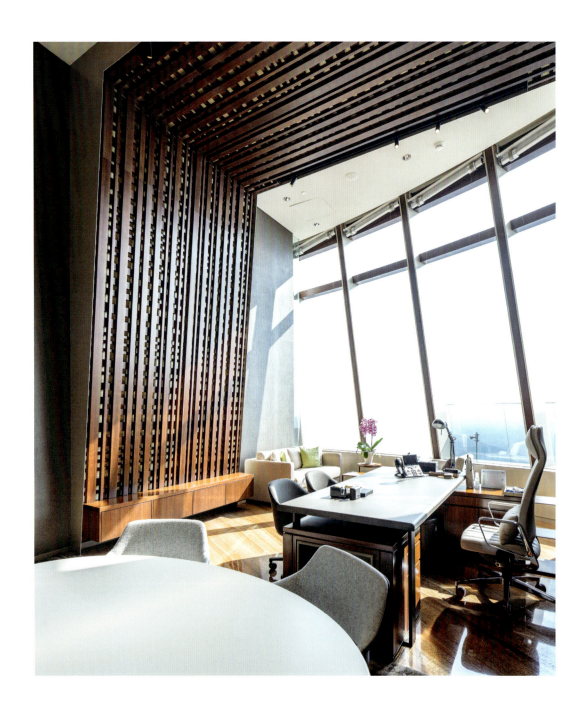

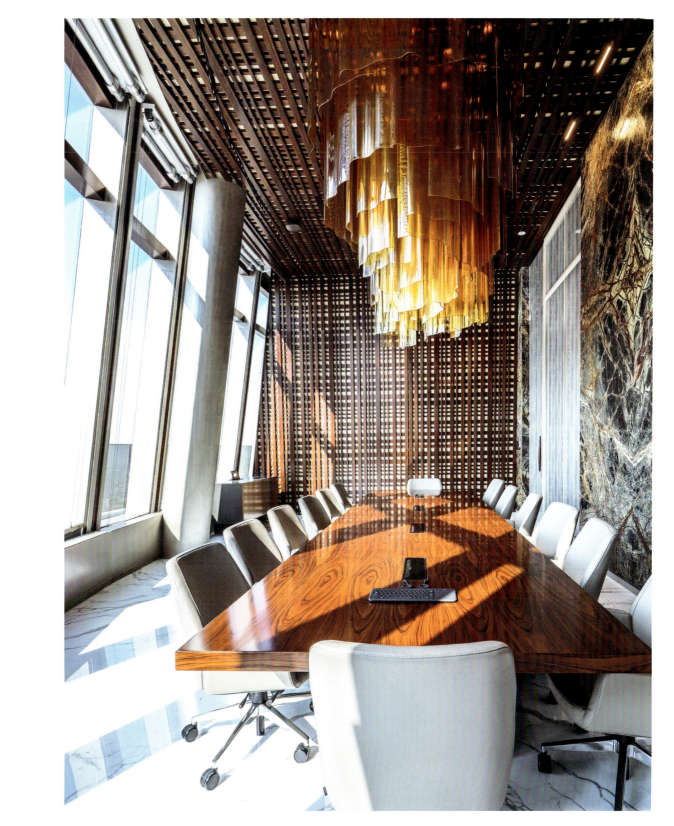

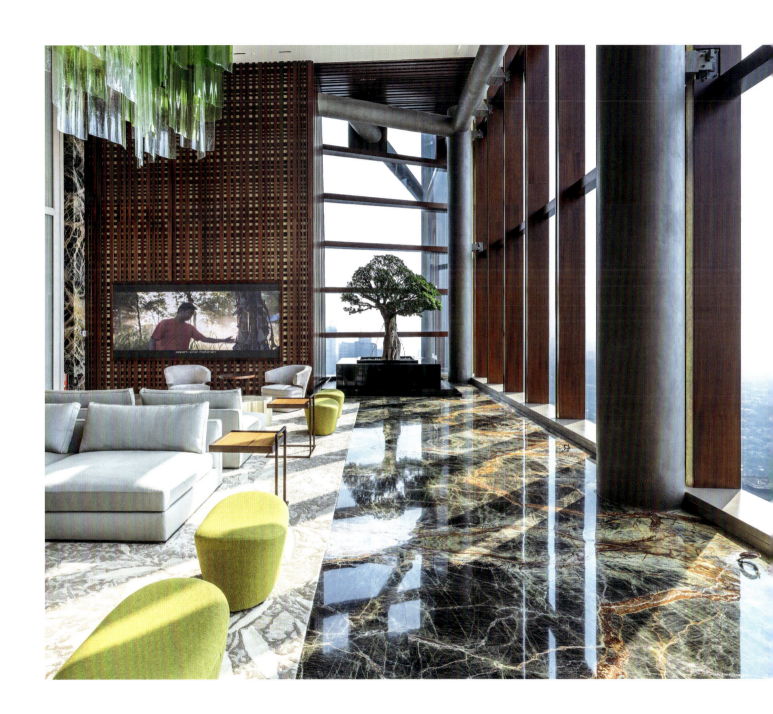

layer noun or verb

lay·er 'lā-ər

noun | plural: layers

1   one that lays something (such as a worker who lays brick or a hen that lays eggs)
2   one thickness, course, or fold of a material or substance or piece laid or lying over a surface or under another
3   an idea or system that may have many different features or levels
4   a branch or shoot of a plant that roots while still attached to the parent plant, or a a plant developed by layering

verb | layers; layering; layered

1   to propagate (a plant) by means of layers, for instance by placing a layer on top of another, or to form or arrange in layers
2   to arrange into layers
3   to separate into layers
4   to form out of superimposed layers
5   to form roots where a stem comes in contact with the ground

layered adjective

lay·erd 'la-erd

1   something arranged in more than one layer
2   something that is made or exists in layers
3   used to describe something that is complicated or interesting, denoting many different levels or features

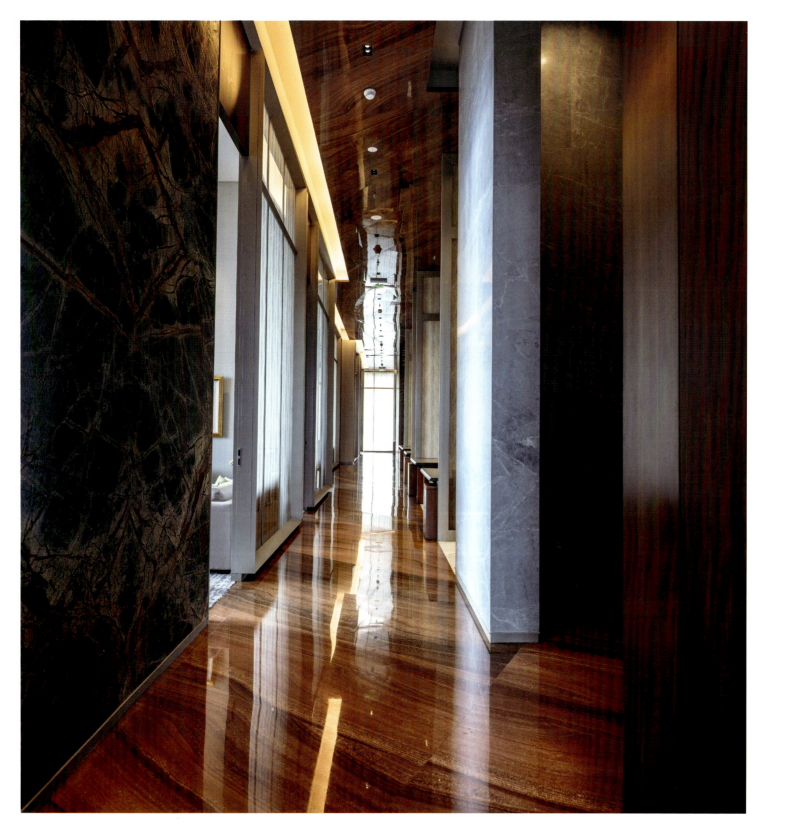

HONORING HERITAGE

welcome verb, interjection, adjective, or noun

wel·come ˈwel-kəm

verb | welcoming; welcomed

1 to greet the coming of (a person) hospitably and with
   kindliness, courtesy, or cordiality
2 to accept with pleasure the occurrence or presence of
3 to receive or regard as welcome an action, decision, or
   situation: *she welcomed the change*

interjection

1 a kindly word of expression used to greet wanted guests or
   newcomers upon arrival: *welcome to my home*

adjective

1 gladly received into one's presence or companionship, as one
   whose coming gives pleasure: *a welcome visitor*
2 agreeable, as something coming, or occuring, or experienced:
   a welcome rest
3 willingly permitted or admitted: *she was welcome to come and go*
4 used used as a reply to an expression of thanks: *you're welcome*

noun

1 a kindly greeting or reception, usually upon arrival: *to give one a
   warm welcome*
2 the state of being welcome

remember verb | remembering; remembered

re·mem·ber ri-ˈmem-bər

1 to bring to mind, still have an idea of, or think of again

2 to recall it back into the mind by an act of effort or memory

3 to have (something, or someone) come into the mind again

4 to remind (someone) to possess or exercise the faculty of memory of an idea, thing, or person

5 to keep in mind for attention or consideration

6 to retain in the memory, bear in mind

7 to convey greetings from someone

8 record, commemorate

social adjective or noun

so·cial ˈsō-shəl

adjective

1 relating to, devoted to, or characterized by friendly companionship or relations
2 friendly or sociable, as persons or the disposition, spirit
3 marked by or passed in pleasant companionship with friends or associates
4 of, relating to, or designed for sociability, such as a physical or virtual space
5 of or relating to society, or its organization, or the welfare of human beings as members of society; not solitary
6 living, or disposed to live, in companionship with others, tending to form cooperative and interdependent relationships with others or in a community, rather than in isolation
7 relating to leisure activities that involve meeting other people: *a social club*
8 a needing of companionship; gregarious, interdependent
9 being such in social situations

noun

1 friendly or sociable, as persons inclined to associate with or be in the company of others: *she's social*
2 the formation and transformation of social life, or customs, or institutions: *social evolution* or *social development*
3 relating to society or to the way society is organized
4 the entire inherited pattern of cultural activity present in a society: *social heritage*

relax verb | relaxes; relaxing; relaxed

re·lax ri-ˈlaks

1 to make or become less tense, stiff, firm, or rigid; grow milder

2 to make less strict, severe, or stringent, as rules, discipline

3 to diminish the force of

4 to treat (hair) chemically in order to relax curls

5 to become lax, weak, or loose; rest

6 to become less intense or severe

7 of a muscle or muscle fiber; to become inactive and lengthen

8 to cast off social restraint, nervous tension, or anxiety

9 to seek rest or recreation

10 to attain equilibrium following the abrupt removal of some
    influence (such as light, high temperature, or stress)

MATERIALITY

collection noun

col·lec·tion kə-ˈlek-shən

1 a set of objects or things deliberately or systematically acquired, usually over a period of time

2 an accumulation of objects (specimens, photographs, paintings, prints, and so on) gathered for study, comparison, or exhibition, or as a hobby

3 an organized assemblage of objects or specimens acquired and maintained for public or private reference

4 an anthology of poems, stories, articles, or other writings

5 a sum of money gathered for a (usually charitable) cause

6 group, aggregate

7 the act or process of collecting: *collection of* data, taxes, and so on

8 a set of apparel designed for sale especially in a particular season: *fashion collection*

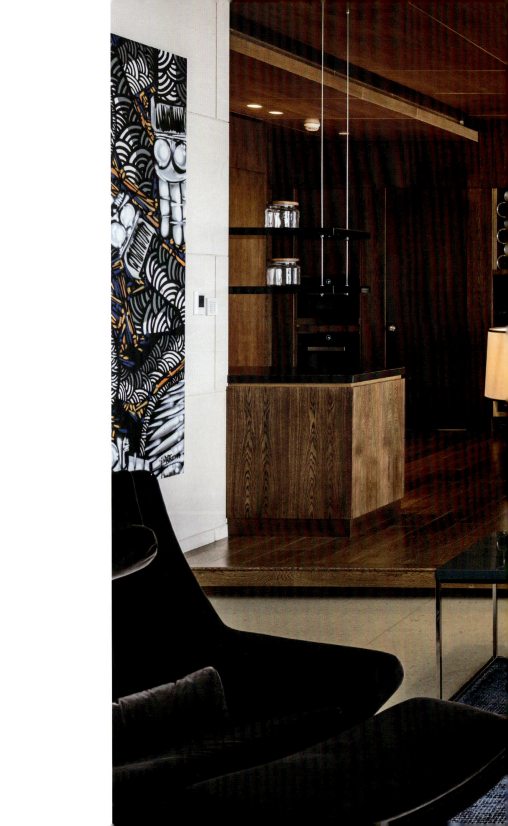

texture noun or verb

tex·ture ˈteks-chər

noun | plural: textures

1 the quality or style resulting from composition: *the texture of her life*
2 the visual or tactile surface characteristics and appearance of something, such as the skin structure and surface of any work of art, such as a painting or sculpture
3 a composite of the elements of prose or poetry
4 in music, a combination of timbres, or tone colors; or the pattern of relationships between the parts of a musical form or sound, such as those created by tones or lines played or sung together: *harmonic texture*
5 the characteristic disposition of something composed of closely interwoven or intertwined elements, such as threads or strands, or the structure formed by the threads of a fabric
6 the essential quality of something, especially as conveyed to the touch in the way that it feels, in how smooth or rough it is (for instance)

verb | texturing; textured

1 to give a distinctive, desired, or particular (often rough, course, or grainy) texture to
2 to make a texture by adding either something tactile or changing the composition to something: *for texture*

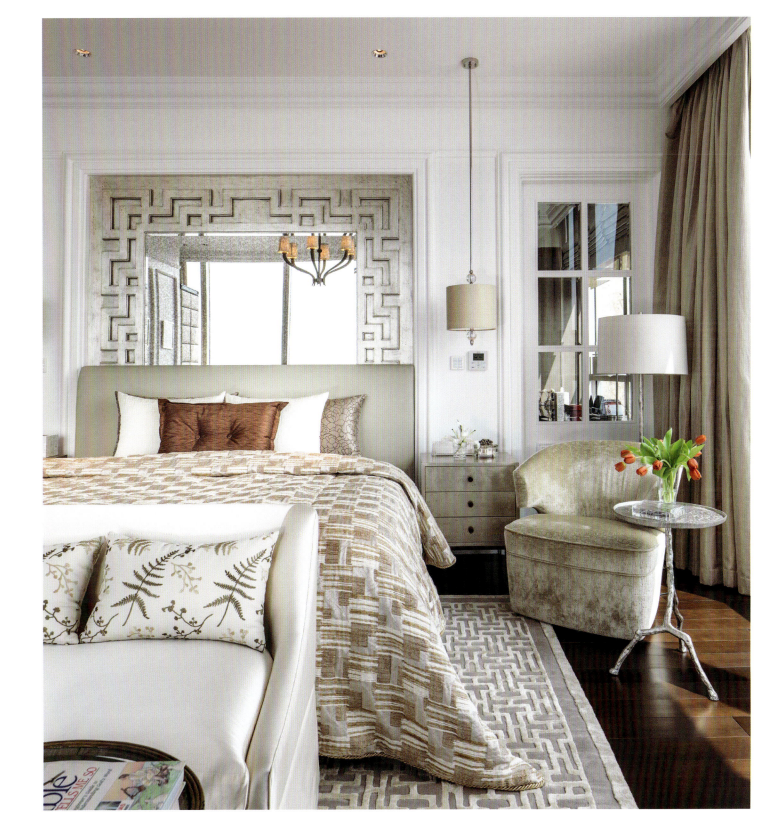

PALETTE

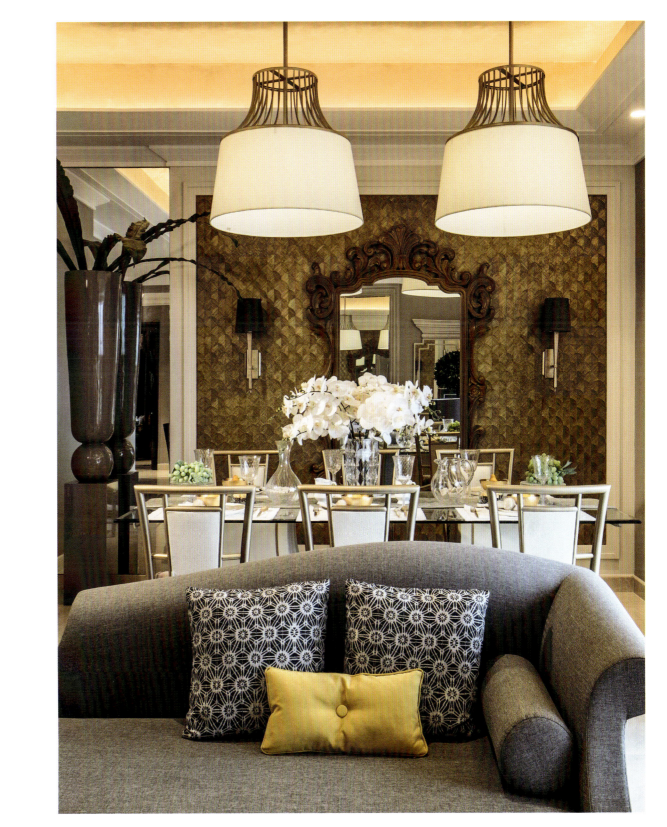

hue noun | plural: hues

ˈhyü

1 a gradation of color or tint; the property that enables an observer to distinguish color per the spectrum as red, yellow, green, blue, and so on, or an intermediate between any contiguous pair of these colors (excludes white, black, and shades of gray)

2 the overall character or appearance to the mind, of complexion, form, or aspect

reflection noun

re·flec·tion ri-ˈflek-shən

1 the act or instance of reflecting

2 in physics, the process by which the return of light, heat, or sound waves are sent back from a surface and do not pass through it

3 something produced by reflecting, such as an image or color given back by a reflecting surface; or an effect produced by an influence

4 an often obscure or indirect criticism; reproach

5 a thought, idea, or opinion formed, or a remark made as a result of meditation or careful thought about a particular subject

6 careful consideration of some subject matter, idea, or purpose

7 something revealed about an attitude or situation, such as comments or writings that express someone's ideas about that idea or situation

8 the state of being reflected

9 an image that one can see usually in a mirror, on water, or in glass

Beauty is the quality or qualities that give pleasure to the senses or mind. These qualities are both tangible and intangible, creating a visual and perceptual experience that stirs an emotional response. This collection of work showcases beauty in architecture and design. We are on a continual exploration of how to make beautiful buildings, spaces, and objects, always developing our knowledge and experience of what is beautiful, as it is manifested and perceived in different ways.

While some architects work in one style, continuously refining and perfecting it, I love to explore different styles and to learn, discover, and evolve. I grew up in America and have traveled, lived, and studied around the world. Now in Indonesia for more than thirty years, I bring this broad understanding and perspective to PAI's work, while always being inspired by and embracing Indonesian culture, tradition, and the sharing of ideas. It's this fusion and approach that sets my work apart.

The words you've encountered in this book are some of the ways in which we manifest beauty in our work. These words reflect both the physical and sensorial qualities in a design. Sometimes you see them, such as the materiality, palette, and light. Sometimes you feel them, such as anticipation and transitions. These qualities are all highly considered and carefully layered to create residential, commercial, and hospitality spaces that we characterize as "comfort luxury" and that have a positive emotional affect. They are spaces for people to feel at home; oases to enjoy after a long day.

Crafting the spaces comes from thoughtful consideration of the journey through a house, and what people will see and feel as they **transition** from space to space—from **public** to **private**, from collective spaces to **sanctuaries**.

At Residence at Prapañca (*see* Collective Spaces and Sanctuaries: Public), an imposing monumental façade conceals a quiet sanctuary. The solid granite wall closes the house to the street. But once inside, the house is open and transparent, as glass walls wrap around the central pool, providing each room with views across the water and through the house. These rooms are like pavilions floating on top of the water, sparkling with light and **reflections**. This subtle play of light and shadow, the contrast of weight and suspension, and the balance of solidity and lightness creates tension and a dramatic architectural expression.

The journey through the house, always alongside the pool, is not only a physical transition, but also a sensory transition. The end point, or resting point, is the bedroom suite—a quiet retreat and refuge deep in the house, away from the street. The walk-through robe wraps around a spa and shower, where water rains down from a skylit shower head and there is a view to the garden beyond. The materials also shift from softly textured parchment-like granite in collective spaces to warm timber in private spaces, further creating the sense of enclosure, sanctuary, and transition.

We orchestrate the experience to begin the moment people enter a property or building. Spaces are sequenced to evoke **anticipation** for what will be revealed and the expectation of discovering more.

Residence at Hang Lekir (*see* Collective Spaces and Sanctuaries: Anticipation) is a vast family compound that is both private and public. The property is a retreat for the influential family, and it has a ballroom for hosting public occasions. For visitors attending a special event, the choreographed arrival sequence heightens the anticipation as they pass through layers of security before navigating through the expansive garden to the house. They arrive to the solid teak front door, carved by a local artist, and then enter a double-height skylit foyer with a shimmering onyx screen. They continue through the entry, drawn in by views of the garden beyond. These glimpses of another space maintain people's desire for discovering more—and they are always rewarded.

For the family, the composition of house and garden offers anticipation and discovery. The architecture is evocative of the Prairie style: long and linear with large overhangs, and surrounded by landscaped garden and pools. We framed views out of and through the house to showcase the garden at different viewpoints in beautiful ways.

At PAI, we're recognized for our sensitivity to proportions. We draw from the classical language of architecture to create harmony, and then finish and furnish rooms with originality and ambience. While Residence at Prapañca is bold, modernist architecture, Residence at Widya Chandra (*see* Capturing Light) is a classical house with modern expression. We designed the interiors and collaborated on the architecture to capture light and create flow from room to room, always thinking about the journey and the spaces **in-between**.

Drawing on classical architecture and the traditional vernacular, the materials include travertine stone, marble floors, and wood-paneled walls, while the aluminum windows and awnings, exposed brick, and sweeping staircase with timber-lined walls inject a modern touch. We worked closely with the client to select furniture from America and Europe as well as local and original pieces, and we varied the palettes between rooms—from light and soft to dark and heavy. This modulation imbues the interior with contrast and depth and offers variety and richness throughout the house.

These spaces and materials also capture light, which is key to all our designs. As sunlight hits different textures, the colors subtly change, and rooms take on different characters as the light and shadows shift from morning to evening. The more finely tuned a space is for light, the richer and more beautiful it is.

Of course, in Indonesia, we need to balance the sunlight and heat. We design high ceilings not only for a luxurious sense of space, but to let more natural light inside, and to draw up hot air to help cool a room. At Residence at Widya Chandra, we also designed an atrium courtyard to bring more light, glazing, and modulation into the center of the house and to showcase the client's superb sculpture.

Mother nature is the star of the show at Sanna Ubud (*see* Framing Nature) in Bali, where the luxury retreat is set amid a lush tropical rainforest, providing guests with an immersive escape. We seamlessly integrated nature and the local architectural tradition to give visitors insight into the Balinese artistic and spiritual approach to design and life. The roof, floor, and traditional columns frame nature, and the beds and seating are positioned for guests to relax and look out to the magnificent views, establishing a true connection with the landscape that surrounds them.

When we design residences and hotels, we imagine and conceive dream homes and villas where residents and guests can relax, enjoy their daily routines, spend time with family, and find sanctuary from the world outside. When we design commercial projects, we develop spaces that embody the values or narrative of the business. Consequently, the design can be more conceptual—a visual representation of the company.

For the Astra International Office (*see* Transitional Stories) at the crown of the Menara Astra tower, we conceived the three levels as a transitional story. Each floor is a different **layer** of a great banyan tree, which represents growth and strength, symbolically protecting and nourishing those around it.

The lower level is the **roots**, as the legacy of Astra has created a long history and a stable foundation. To depict this, we had marble laser cut to create the dramatic imagery of root elements snaking across the floor. The middle level (and arrival floor) is the trunk of the banyan tree with wood-look marble on the floor and ceiling. One block of marble is sliced in two to mirror each other and create the impression of being in the middle of a tree trunk. The metaphor continues in the slats of wood that wrap around the walls and ceilings, as well as is in the branch-like lighting pendants and the timber boardroom table with marble inlay.

The upper level is the canopy, where the opulent green, brown, and yellow marble is intricately veined, evocative of the branches and leaves of a tree. A "nest" housing the library is suspended from the 23-foot-high (7-meter-high) ceiling and has a voluminous cloud-like light, reminiscent of the Indonesian mist.

Indonesia and its symbolism, culture, climate, and traditions have inspired me since the day I arrived here. Designing the Astra International Office was an opportunity to bring symbolism to life, while designing the Hermitage Hotel (*see* Honoring Heritage) in Menteng was an in-depth exploration into Indonesian and Dutch colonial architecture and decorative arts.

I first visited the building—originally the Dutch colonial telecommunications office—in the early 2000s when it was abandoned. It was facing demolition until the present owner bought it and turned into a luxury hotel. In designing the interiors, we reimagined the 1930s to honor the heritage of the art deco building. From the reception and breakfast room, where guests are **welcomed**, to the **social** spaces—the restaurant, cigar bar, private dining room, and rooftop bar—to the bedroom suites, where they **relax**, we infused the Hermitage with the essence of Dutch colonial design to create beautiful spaces and a memorable atmosphere that evokes another place and time.

The original rooms were plain with high ceilings, and natural light streamed through the windows. We integrated intricate paneling and detailing to walls and doors, creating geometries and rhythm that draws visitors through a space. We also draped fabrics, layered textures, and contrasted light and dark materials, providing a rich and elegant background for furnishings and objects that **remember** and reimagine Menteng in the 1930s: antique pieces, original chairs, hand-crafted Javanese furniture, brass lamps, and storm lanterns for pendants. We then adorned rooms with hand paintings, porcelain, batiks, and more, to elaborate on the narrative of a Dutch colonial building transformed into an unforgettable five-star boutique hotel.

Materiality is vital to creating these beautiful spaces that offer comfort and luxury. At the Apartments at Keraton (*see* Materiality), it was also one way in which we differentiated two luxury homes—distinguishing two generations of the same family. One is for the parents; the other is for their adult children; and each apartment reflects the occupants and their style. We achieved this distinction, and the different aesthetics and atmospheres, through materiality, **texture**, and the **collection** of furniture.

The parents' residence is mature and classic and captures their love of colonial architecture. Architraves and columns frame grand openings and modulate spaces. The furniture is classic and soft; the color palette is tonal with orange accents; and the objects have voluptuous forms. In contrast, the children's residence is contemporary, edgier, and more dynamic. Different spaces are defined by variation in the floor levels and materials, and the furniture is contemporary and modern, with sleeker and sharper forms and textures.

We similarly focused on the palette at Amala show home (*see* Palette). Designed to be visually interesting and stimulating, the bold **hues**, forms, and patterns create an immersive space that captures attention. High-color accents, gold-curtain backdrops, and textured and graphic wallpapers, bed coverings, and rugs contribute to a rich composition that proved to be popular with visitors. We also crafted the lighting and **reflections** to create a greater sense of space and depth within the apartment.

These projects represent beauty in some of its infinite forms. As we look forward, PAI will continue to explore the qualities of creating beauty and the many different expressions that manifest from our architecture and design approach. We'll continue to grow and evolve as designers, as we imagine and craft beautiful homes for our clients, and they bring new ideas that inspire us. We'll always chase the ideas that make their dreams real.

The art of architecture and interior design offers so many ways of expressing beauty, shelter, and home. By layering the tangible and intangible qualities of design, we can create a rich and luxurious experience that offers contentment, tranquility, inspiration, surprise, and many other emotions of feeling at home.

THOMAS ELLIOTT
Director of Design, PAI (PT. Paramita Abirama Istasadhya)

ABOUT

translate verb | translating; translated

trans·late tran(t)s-'lāt

1 to express the sense of a word, sentence, or speech, and so on, into one's own or another language or dialect

2 to do this as a profession or act as a translator

3 to practice translation or make a translation

4 to undergo a translation

5 to transfer or turn from one set of symbols into another; transcribe

6 to express in other terms and especially different words; paraphrase

7 to express in more simpler, comprehensible terms; explain, interpret

8 to bear, remove, carry, or change from one place, position, state, condition, form, or appearance to another; transfer, transform

9 to convey to heaven or to a nontemporal condition without death; transform

10 to transfer or infer the significance of (words, gestures, symbols, and so on)

11 in theology, to transfer (a person) from one place or plane of existence to another, as from earth to heaven

12 in mathematics, to subject to mathematical translation (by moving a shape left, right, up, or down)

13 in biochemistry, to subject genetic information to translation; to transform the molecular structure into a polypeptide chain by means of the information stored in the genetic code

14 in physics, to cause (a body) to move so that all its parts travel in the same direction, in other words, without sideways rotation or angular displacement

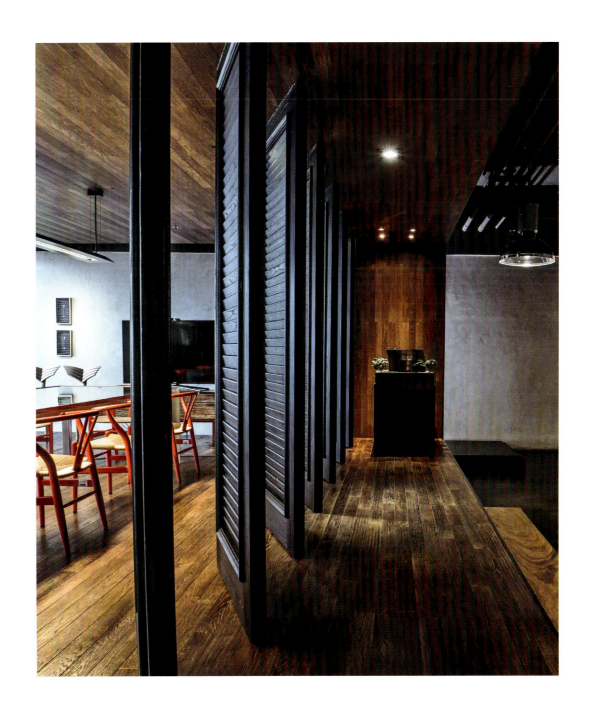

create verb | creating; created

cre·ate kre-ˈāt

1   to cause it to happen or exist; to give rise to
2   to invest, constitute, or appoint (a person) with a new form, office, or rank
3   to evolve from one's thought or imagination
4   to produce or invent through imaginative skill and design
5   to be the first to represent (a part or role)

Acknowledgments

No architectural construction is a single person's act. It is by its very nature a collaboration. Those daring or naive to put forward ideas of form or expression of volumes for habitation rely heavily on the support of many other disciplines. This acknowledgment is an attempt to say thank you to those people.

To my clients, who trust me to create.

To my business partner, Lanny Ridjab, who gives me room to think.

To my collaborative team at PAI, who suffer through my moods.

To the many creative consultants, whose insight and advice make each endeavor great.

To the suppliers of materials and equipment, whose expertise is always necessary.

Of course, to my family, whose love and patience are the rock of my existence.

Company Profile

Thomas Elliott and PAI have a longstanding reputation for producing excellent design across residential, hospitality, hotel, commercial, and master planning projects. While our work is primarily in Indonesia, we also design projects for clients in Singapore, China, and the United States.

Our marketing and operational director, Lanny Ridjab, founded PAI in 1986, and architect and designer Thomas Elliott, director of design, joined in 1992. PAI's team of sixty-five-plus architects and designers **translate** a client's brief and vision to **create** their dream home, hotel, or office.

The modern industrial style of our studio, with brick, metal, and wood, is evocative of a contemporary loft, despite being in an office tower. As with every project that PAI designs, natural light and outdoor views are crucial for our environment and employees' wellbeing. Everyone has a connection to the view for daylight and to see the outside atmosphere, whether it's sunny, bright, rainy, or dark. The open-plan space has two platforms that vary the floor level and provide raised workstations with more access to light and views. For desks facing inward, a mirror installed on the core wall reflects the office and window and enhances the light and sense of space in the studio. The prayer room, warehouse, pantry, and server room are positioned near the core of the building, where they don't block natural light from entering work areas. Our office also provides a window for everyone passing through or waiting in the lift lobby on the twenty-first floor. A deliberate gap at the edge of the meeting room continues the window along the room.

Like us, our clients appreciate beautiful design, and we have great satisfaction and pride in helping make their vision come true.

PAI Team

Thomas Elliott • Lanny Marlitta Ridjab • Umar Sujoko • RM. Ramadana Putera • M. Arief Wibowo • Yustina Dyah Rosari • Wawan Muh. Syawal • Lianny Dwiyanti Samsudin • Tengku Syahrita Muchdin

Ade Kurnia • Adela Maulidya • Afrido Ardhana • Alfin Seftian • Arga Artistika • Arianto • Arya Birendra • Budhi Sukma • Christia Wulan Febrida • Cut Ela Hajjah Apriliani • Dani Fardial Utama • Daniella Sudjana • Dewi Kartika • Didi Supriadi • Dimas Aditya • Dyah Nisita Rahmi • Endah Husnul Khotimah • Evy Kumala • Febri Wahyu Kurniawan • Fida Windari Dewi • Helly Krisnandriono • Hendro Cahyo Saputro • I Wayan Putra Sanjaya • Imansyah • Inayati Utami • Indramewaty • Ineke Marta • Ismat • Ivan Latovana • Iwan Nurwondo • Jamaludin • Joko Suwanto • Mansell Mulyadi • Maria Caecilia A • Ramlan Gunawan • Richard Orlando • Risman • Sabar Suherman • Sandra Desi • Satria Oktafitrianta • Sony Dias Tri Wibowo • Sri Wahyudi • Sudijat • Sudiman • Suharto • Suyadi • Syailendra Islamsyah • Tedy Luntagiri • Teguh Prihatin • Timothy Ariel Andana • Tisna Nuryadin Athar • Tomi Rendra Pratama • Tri Pratiwi Handayani • Triyatno Susilo • Turohman • Wibowo Wibisono • Yenny Hirawati • Yohanna Cindy Vania Djaja • Yosef Rendra

Consultants

STRUCTURAL PT. Davy Sukamta & Partners • I Ketut Yasa Bagiarta • PT. Hadi & Associates • PT. Maxim Gritama • PT. Reliance Consulting Engineers • PT. Stadin Strukturindo Konsultan **LIGHTING** PT. Litac • PT. Lumina Group Prabashvara • PT. Realta Kencana • PT. Hadi Komara & Associates **ARCHITECTURE CONTRACTORS** PT. Arcon Partama Cipta • PT. Concreate Anugerah Abadi • PT. Kencana Sewu Persada • PT. Sigmatech Contractor • PT. Zetta Konstruksi **INTERIOR CONTRACTORS** PT. Bika Parama Cipta • CV. Bukit Mas Karya Konstruksi (BMKK) • PT. Caturgriya Naradipa • PT. Citra Cipta Bika • PT. Gitalaras • PT. Idea Kreatama Mandiri • PT. Saniharto Enggalhardjo **MECHANICAL, ELECTRICAL & PLUMBING** PT. Hantaran Prima Mandiri • PT. Maxim Gritama • PT. Meinhardt Indonesia • PT. Meltech Consultindo Nusa • PT. Metakom Pranata • PT. Mitra Bahana Engineering **LANDSCAPING** PT. Alamcipta Nuansa Hijau • Belt Collins • Bensley Design • PT. Eschol Swarna Bhumi • PT. Intaran Design • La Palma Landscape • SHL Asia • Wijaya Garden

Suppliers

A • Anoma Wood • Antonangeli • Arclinea • Artkey • Asahimas • Atap Teduh Lestari • **B** • B&B Italia • Bika Living • Bisazza • Bottega&Artisan • Bottega Veneta Home • PT. Bloomfils International (Miele) • Bocci • Boffi Kitchen • Blackwood • **C** • Calissa Home • Citatah • CJ Trading • Clipsal • Creaton • **D** • de Sede • PT. Dharmawan Wiganda • DCWéditions • **E** • PT. Estica International (Technal) • Eztu Glass • **F** • Fagetti • Ferro Aluminia • Flexform • Flos • **G** • Gampang Ingat • Giorgetti • Grohe • **H** • Habitus Concept • Häfele Indonesia • Hubbardton Forge • **I** • Il Sogno Aluminium • Infissi-Magran Group • Intermulindo Utama • Interni Asia • **J** • Jung Electric Indonesia • **K** • Kitchen Culture • Kohler Indonesia • Kuda Laut Mass • **L** • Lasvit Indonesia • Laflo • Legrand Indonesia • Lakkasta • Luceplan • **M** • Maestro Lamp • Marga Agung • Magran Group • Minotti • MM Galleri • MOIE • **O** • Otiima • Owens Corning • **P** • Panasonic Indonesia • Prodotti Indonesia • **Q** • Quantum Marble & Granite • **R** • Rita Widagdo • Rimadesio • Roche Bobois • **S** • Sans Souci • Seni Mulia • Stella Mobili • Surya Toto Indonesia • **T** • Tuscany • **V** • Vastuhome • Victoria + Albert

FORWARD

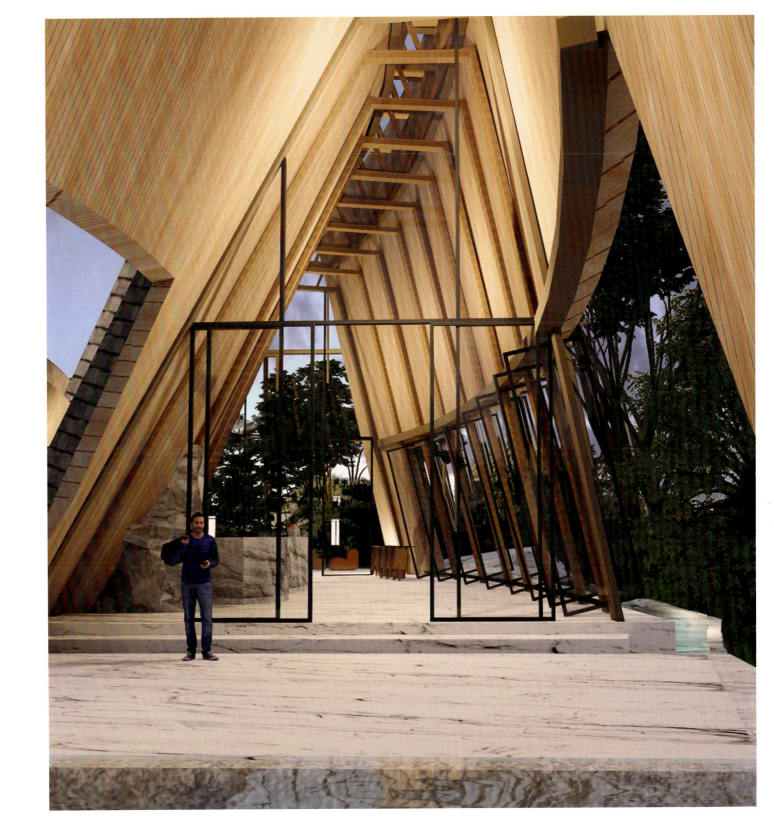

Published in Australia in 2024 by
The Images Publishing Group Pty Ltd
ABN 89 059 734 431

Offices

MELBOURNE

Waterman Business Centre
Suite 64, Level 2 UL40
1341 Dandenong Road
Chadstone, Victoria 3148
Australia
Tel: +61 3 8564 8122

NEW YORK

6 West 18th Street 4B
New York, NY 10011
United States
Tel: +1 212 645 1111

SHANGHAI

6F, Building C, 838 Guangji Road
Hongkou District, Shanghai 200434
China
Tel: +86 021 31260822

books@imagespublishing.com
www.imagespublishing.com

Copyright © Thomas Elliott (text); photographer/s as indicated 2024
The Images Publishing Group Reference Number: 1693

All photography is attributed to Thomas Elliott (© 2024)

A catalogue record for this book is available from the National Library of Australia

Title: Thomas Elliott: Directions
ISBN: 9781864709728

This title was commissioned in IMAGES' Melbourne office and produced as follows:
Editorial Georgia (Gina) Tsarouhas, Rebecca Gross **Production & art direction** Nicole Boehringer

Printed on 157gsm Chinese OJI matt art paper (FSC®) in China by Artron Art Group